A CAT IN THE TROPICS.

BASED ON A TRUE STORY

BY MARK DEANE-SMITH.

Copyright : Mark Deane-Smith.

2015.

Original Photography by

Mark Deane-Smith.

Printed by CreateSpace,

an Amazon.com company.

This book is dedicated to my parents Brian and Yvonne Deane-Smith, for their appreciation of animals and the environment which we all share.

1. THE KITTY STORY.

Our family lived on a rural farm in Koah, near Mareeba, in North Queensland, near the Barron River. Kitty was born in a boat that was being painted by one of our neighbours who lived near the river. Her mother was a feral Tabby, and had decided to have her kittens in a safe place. There were six kittens, and the owner of the boat had seen them there at night, but by the morning they had gone. The mother must have spent many hours moving the six kittens to another place. She would carry them one at a time in her mouth, carefully watching all the time. The next day he saw them in a log in the bush, on another property.

The following day, the mother cat moved the kittens again, up to a large shed on a farm property. The woman who lived there saw them, and she put some food and water nearby for the mother. The next day she found one kitten missing, and two others dead. A snake, or possibly a Monitor lizard had killed them. The mother cat then moved the three remaining kittens under the farm house, which was built on stilts, and tried to befriend the owner, looking for food. There were two black and white kittens, and one tabby. A few days went by, and the kittens opened their eyes and started to move about. The mother cat then moved the kittens back into the bush again. Feral cats often move their families every few days as a safety plan. Unfortunately, another kitten vanished, and a male kitten was found on a pathway, sick with a parasite tick. The owner of the farm took the kitten to the Vet, and it was saved. It then came to live in the farm house, and it was a very happy puss, and much loved. The mother cat took the other kitten, a black and white female, back under the house. By the time this kitten was six months old, she still lived with the mother under the house. She played with her brother, but was quite wild. It was decided that we could have her, so she came to stay at our house.

She was very difficult for a while, and caused quite a lot of damage. We called her Kitty, as she answered to that name. She settled down, and was really lovely with four white socks, a white mask and white underneath. The rest of her coat was black, with very thick fur.

After a few weeks, we decided to take her to the Vet to have her speyed. To our surprise, the Vet found that she was pregnant. We had thought she was too young and small to have kittens, but we had to wait until she gave birth. She did not want to use a box we made for her, and instead went under a chest in the study. It was very cramped, but she produced six kittens. Two were stillborn, and a third one died on the first night. She then moved the remaining three under a bookcase in another room, and every two or three days took them somewhere else in the house. She washed and fed them, and we befriended them. One day a Taipan, which is a kind of venomous snake, came in a small gap in the door from the porch, and slithered down the hallway towards the cats. Mark saw it, and it turned around, and went straight out the same gap again. It went to the fishpond, had a drink, and then took off. The Taipan is considered to be about the 3rd most venomous snake in the world. We quite like snakes, but of course we don't want them just marching into the house!

2. The Kittens Growing Up.

We started to give the kittens some meals, and soon found out that they don't necessarily like the same types of food. Kitty was no problem, she ate cat meat as well as dry food and drank milk. Conrad and Cleo also ate meat, however, Tiga refused the meat completely. We tried some raw meat, mostly chicken, and this was accepted. Great! She also ate some raw fish and tinned tuna, but preferred the chicken meat. We didn't want them to become reliant on hunting, so it was important to establish a routine. Generally, a meal for breakfast, and a meal at about three or four o'clock worked the best.

The kittens began exploring outside. We had a dog, named Leo, who was an excellent watch dog, and he only had to bark and the cats went scooting under the beds, or came back inside the house. We also had free-range chickens and Guinea Fowls, and they all got along fine with each other. The kittens were curious about everything around them. Interestingly, they didn't mind walking in the small pond or getting a bit wet, especially Cleo.

It was fascinating watching how the kittens developed, as usually people have one cat. Mum tried to find homes for them, but no one was keen to have a "stray" puss. So eventually we decided to keep them. There was one male and two females. We called the male Conrad, and he was the largest of the group. He had some white markings, but was mostly dark with beautiful swirls of tan making a patterned coat. He had grey-blue eyes when he was younger, and an elegant head. The two little females were smaller. One we called Cleo and she was lovely with silky fur and black and white markings. She was very venturesome and liked to explore around the property. She had no fear and liked to climb everything including the roof, but then she pretended that she needed help to get down?!

The third kitten was small with thick fur like Kitty, and she was a Tabby with a small white patch under her chin. We used to live in Indonesia, so we called her "Tiga", meaning "Three". She had bright staring eyes, and loved to "wash" the other cats, including her mum. She always seemed frightened, but then did what she wanted.

Clockwise from left to right :
Conrad, Cleo and Tiga.

"What are all these books doing here?"

By the time the kittens were two years old, they were very much part of our family and had developed individual personalities. Conrad liked to come inside in the evening and sit on Mum's lap while she was reading. Cleo liked exploring or being with Mark, while Tiga liked sleeping on beds. Kitty liked being on top of the pantry, or the fridge. Sometimes they all went outside to explore. They have very much become part of our lives.

Conrad, Cleo, Tiga and Kitty.

8.

For the cats, and especially as kittens, there was plenty to do around the property. We had wide open lawns to run on, and several trees and small gardens around the house. Kitty was already adept at hunting. Some people may worry about cat's habits of hunting, and disturbing the wildlife. Certainly in the wild, they have to hunt to survive. However, given the extremely low survival rate, at least around our area, they will hardly become very populous. More likely they will struggle to survive, with many predators watching them as well. If they are lucky, they might find some people who are sympathetic, and will feed them, and perhaps adopt them.

That said, we were more than happy to have the cats around the house, as we had a real problem with mice, as well as rats. They have an amazing ability to chew things - containers, boxes, even wires. Strangely enough, when Kitty arrived, they mostly vanished back into the bush...

We have a number of resident Geckos in the house, which are good to have around, as they eat quite a lot of insects, including cockroaches. Unfortunately, the cats also took an interest in them. We spend a lot of time telling them not to chase the Geckos, but generally they will sit and stare around the room, hoping one will come closer.

The kittens begin to explore, watched closely by Kitty.

The Geckos have learned to be wary of the cats, and always scoot away and hide behind a picture. Outside the cats had fun playing around the fishpond and the Golden palm trees.

The fishpond had a variety of fish in it, as well as a Water lily and some Bullrushes. The cats noticed the fish, but didn't try and catch any of them. We had Rainbowfish, Platys, Gudgeons and some Goldfish, and the pond was nice and deep with steep sides. Frogs and Toads would occasionaly have a swim in it, and we also had some water snakes visit. They didn't bother the fish either, the only danger was from Kookaburras or Kingfishers.

The cats also enjoyed the smaller pond, which was set into a stone wall with a small landscaped garden. It had various plants in it, and at night there were solar lights and lots of small tree frogs set themselves up around it and chirped away for hours.

Top left : Kitty plays with Tiga.
Bottom left : Tiga sits by the pond.
Above : Conrad explores the tussock grass.

3. Learning to climb.

As the kittens grew bigger, they began to learn some of the skills which they might need one day in the future. One of the most important ones was climbing. We had a big Jacaranda tree next to the fishpond, and this proved to be ideal for practicing tree climbing. Everyone seemed to have a natural ability to jump up and hold onto the trunk, and then gradually work their way up the tree.

Sometimes the kittens would jump from branch to branch, chasing each other. They had a lot of fun for a while. Eventually they noticed the roof, and began to climb onto it. Mark put a ladder by the side of the house, and the cats all learned to use it. It was also useful when one of them got "stuck", and wasn't sure how to get down! Mostly they got up and down themselves.

The cats liked sitting outside in the sun, but came to shelter when it rained. There are roughly four seasons here, a Spring, Summer, which is hot - around thirty degrees celsius is about average - and is also known as the "Cyclone season", and Autumn which is called the "flood" period when the rains come, followed by a short winter during which the temperatures vary a lot, and can get quite cool. Most of the year is dry, and we rely on the river to pump our water.

Unless the river is flooded, we use a small pump to transfer water to our two tanks, which are situated near the house and next to a large Mango tree. The free-range hens and roosters use the tree as a roost at night. They fly up into the tree and hop from branch to branch, and the Guinea fowls, who arrived more recently, now do the same. We also have a Peacock which actually belongs to our neighbours, but has set himself up here on our property, and he also sits in the tree, and we sometimes have some Fruit Bats, also called Flying Foxes which roost high up near the top.

The Flying Foxes were particularly common during the Mango season in the early summer, and spent hours raiding the tree just after dark, causing plenty of commotion in the tree and dropping Mangoes everywhere, including on top of our water tanks. They also ate seeds from the palm trees, and made a real mess on the ground. They often argued about who should be the first to eat something. The cats were interested, but always stayed well away from the bats. We also had small bats which ate insects in the evening, as well as the Frogmouth birds and some Owls which came to have a look around. Frilled Lizards are common here in the summer, and will climb a tree if you approach them. There were some wild pigs in the bush, as well as the occasional wild horses or "Brumbies", and even some wild cattle. Dingoes were less common but were also in the bush. I saw two in the long grass once, and sometimes you could see their tracks by the creek, as well as those of other dogs, Wallabies and Kangaroos. We were often busy repairing fences which would inevitably be damaged by something, and the boundary fence had been flattened long ago.

We also had other animals which ended up on the roof. A large Monitor lizard went up there, also a Python, and sometimes tree snakes. The frogs liked hiding there too. There were several different species of frogs around the property, mostly tree frogs. There were also at least two kinds of tree snakes, which were non-venomous.

Conrad exploring the roof.

Sometimes a cat got stuck in the early hours of the morning. Mark would wake up and, hearing the meeows near his bedroom, went outside and helped the cat down from the roof, even in the rain.

Eventually they all learned to climb down the trees near the side of the house, which was a great relief. However, Conrad, who was very strong, could hop off the roof and land on the ground quite easily! Cats have amazingly strong legs, and are very flexible to be able to climb and jump on the trees.

The morning mist finds Conrad, Cleo and Tiga all up on the roof.

4. Growing up on a farm.

The cats had to adapt to all the different conditions, and be able to avoid any problems. One problem which affected many people with animals here are scrub ticks. The cats often sat on the ground in the sand, and unfortunately two of them picked up paralysis ticks. We took them to the vet as soon as we could. The scrub tick can be fatal to both dogs and cats. Fortunately, both kittens survived.

Our farm is on the Atherton Tablelands, which is like a plateau and it has a cooler climate than the coast. However the weather is variable and it can be very hot, or cold with frost on the lawn. The morning mist is common during the winter, and there is a cyclone season which we watch closely. Sometimes there are storms with heavy rain and flooding, which cuts off roads and bridges. When the river floods we rush down to retrieve our pump, or it will be washed away. After a cyclone there is often a lot of debris around, such as fronds from the coconut trees and the palm trees. We then collect these and put them in a pile to dry out before we burn them.

A sunset at Koah.

The morning mist rises over a field.

Most days we get up early, about five or six. In fact, the cats might ensure that we wake up even earlier. There was no cat door at our house, and the result was an endless parade from door to door, back and forth, with various meeows and requests to either leave, or come back in. Mark usually got up late at night to let someone in or out, and the cats quickly learned where and when their best chance was of being heard. Conrad in particular was clever, and began scratching on doors when he wanted to go out. Kitty, Cleo and Tiga usually meeowed quietly. Eventually they found a hole in a screen, and made it wider to be used as a cat door. What fun! Anyway, at least they could get in and out more regularly.

We tried leaving a door open, but unfortunately our free range chickens took advantage of this by coming inside the house. We would then enter the kitchen to find a chook pecking away at the left-overs of the cat's meals. They also went after the sacks of chicken feed, so we had to remember to keep the doors shut. We usually did this anyway because of the snakes.

The Flying Foxes enjoyed visiting our fruit trees, particularly the bananas, as well as the Mandarins and the Pawpaws. There were also a few Cockatoos and other birds which munched away on things. Not much we could do about it, other than accept it as part of nature, though we do understand the damage that the wildlife can cause to people who rely on farming. We put banana bags and nets up to slow the bats down, and this worked quite well.

Fruit bats roost in trees, often in the hundreds, and stay there until their babies have matured. We used to have wild pigs which came onto the lawn and dug huge holes in it, but our dog Leo challenged them, and the result was they went back into the bush, and have not returned in a long time, even though our neighbours have reported pigs on their properties.

Cleo in the potato patch.

Cleo and Kitty with a watermelon.

Tiga and Kitty selling pumpkins...

Still trying to sell this melon!

Some of the year we worked at planting various crops, both to sell and for ourselves to eat. We had several gardens and set up some irrigation systems around the place. The cats were curious, and Cleo in particular would follow Mark out to the fields to see what was going on. She had great fun hopping on the haystacks, hiding in amongst the crops and climbing fence posts. Sometimes Conrad also came out to look, and now and then Kitty followed by Tiga. They especially came out in the evening to explore, or just to sit on the lawn.

We had a variety of crops - sweet potatoes, watermelons, corn, Kassava (or tapioca), bananas, pineapples, pawpaws and pumpkins. It was always a challenge to keep the Kangaroos and rodents as well as the insects away from them. The cats did their part in chasing the rodents away, but we often had dry weather which affected almost everything.

Conrad looks around the garden.

A view to the house from the Eucalypt plantation.

Our property was surrounded by high grass, which locally was called Brackey or "Goat grass". We had some horses, but unfortunately they couldn't eat the grass, only cattle or goats were able to digest it. We spent a considerable amount of time and money keeping the lawn mown, and we cut the longer grass back away from the house. This was a practical thing to do here in particular, because the snakes often used the long grass to move around in during the day. We heard plenty of stories about " huge Taipans or King Browns " roaming across the property, and indeed we saw some ourselves. The best thing was to have a short lawn, because the snakes didn't like being out in the open as much. We also had a small Eucalyptus plantation with trees which were called Messmates. They were originally from New South Wales and were about ten years old.

The cats used to sit and watch the Kangaroos, and also the various birds which came to visit. They were mostly large birds, including Plovers, Egyptian Ibis, Parrots, Honeyeaters, Kookaburras and occasionally some wild Ducks.

A Wallaby.   A pair of Guinea Fowl.

    There were many animals which came to visit our property. Some were just passing through, but others wanted to stay a bit longer. We often had Grey Kangaroos, Red Kangaroos and Agile Wallabies who would gather on the lawn, especially after the rain and at night. Occasionally they would make a noise and "box" each other in a sort of competition. They dug around for roots on the lawn, and made quite a mess. They also ate some of our trees.

    The cats became accustomed to our free-range poultry, and the hens and roosters got used to these new "creatures" which had appeared on the scene. No doubt, they had seen the occasional wild cat prowling around. They may have been a bit nervous if they had chicks, but they seemed to realize that these cats were'nt going to make a meal out of one of them.

    Our birds were called Jungle Fowl, and possibly had originated in Malaysia where settlers had apparently brought some to North Queensland. The Red Jungle Fowl is still common in South-east Asia, but our birds are probably mixed with other kinds, and are generally known as "Modern Game." In the evening they gathered under the big trees and fly up into them to spend the night. This is obviously a good option to escape from predators, such as Dingoes and Pythons which are found in our area. The roosters had a particular crow with four notes in it, and it echoed through the trees. They would crow at any time, in the evening or early morning, not just at daybreak. Then they would begin to form groups with the hens.

Early on I had taught our dog Leo to avoid snakes regardless of what species they were. This had been successful, and he always avoided them. He would often bark loudly if one blundered into the side of his run, or came across the patio. Occasionally a tree snake would climb into the run, but apart from the occasional accident when he almost trod on one there were no major incidents. The cats were curious about the snakes, but also wary. Kitty in particular would hiss as if by instinct if she saw a poisonous snake. But they never tried to attack one.

However, this was not the case with the chooks, or the Guinea Fowl who arrived later. They had to roost up in the trees to avoid predators, as they were on the menu of the Pythons and the Brown tree snake, or "Night Tiger". The tree snakes ate eggs and small chicks, but the Pythons could eat anything, including full-grown Roosters and Guinea Fowls.

Domestic chickens are not strong flyers, and can only manage to stay up for a short time, unlike their wild relatives who can fly for miles. Our birds could only fly a few metres or so, depending on where they were going. They could easily land on the roof of our house, and they were often able to escape a snake by taking off as fast as they could go.

Mark had some experience catching snakes when we had lived overseas in East Africa. He also got some advice from other people who relocate snakes in the bush away from houses. This was the best thing to do so as to avoid the snakes returning to the same huning grounds. At least, that is what we hope for. The alternative is to have the snakes come back over and over again and reduce the population of birds. The snakes are also adept at getting into chicken runs to get a free meal. A bird nesting on the ground is at risk, not only from the snakes. Monitor Lizards are also out there looking for some food too, and the Hawks will take any small chicks that they can. Our chooks have had many battles with the snakes, Hawks and Falcons over the years.

One of our roosters was a bit more defensive than the others, and would even attack a bird of prey at times. We called it the Plantation rooster. One incident I remember was when a hen with seven or so medium sized chicks was attacked by a huge Hawk. The Hawk flew down and the hen flew up, and collided with the Hawk in mid-air. As a result, the Hawk was knocked off balance, and crashed on the ground. The chicks ran screaming everywhere and escaped, while the hen just stood there glaring at the Hawk. The Hawk looked disgusted, it shook it's wings and flew away.

Some of our chooks.

During the day, the cats would usually sit around outside. When we did jobs they would often follow us, or watch from a distance. When the sun got hot, they would find a cool pace and have a nap. They were always alert to any new noises, and would sometimes run away if they were startled by something, or if a visitor came, only to peek out from the side of the house. Some of them would hide under Mum's bed which was a favourite place, or behind the radio in my room.

In the afternoon the cats would often sit near the big Mango tree, watching the chooks looking for food, and getting ready to fly up into the tree to roost at night. The Mango tree was popular because it had many branches, including some quite low, which were easy for the small chicks and guinea fowls to fly up to. We used to watch the mother hens trying to encourage the chicks to fly up into the tree. Eventually they would make it, and would join their parents on a perch and stay there for the night. They would also roost in other smaller trees, but the Mango tree was their favourite.

At nightfall, the cats would watch and listen as the different sounds of the night echoed around them. It was a mysterious time, and there were different animals which came out at night, Kangaroos and Wallabies hopped across the lawn. Bandicoots also appeared, and Frogs and Toads began a chorus of singing. A bird called a Curlew would let out a high-pitched call, and Fruit Bats would screech in the trees. After a while the cats would come back inside one by one, and have a rest.

5. Curiosity and the Cat.

As the kittens grew up they began to explore their surroundings. And as is always the case with most animals, they became conditioned to their environment based on their experiences. Although Kitty was very young when she had them, she still showed a lot of initiative and effort in rearing her kittens.

First she led them outside their room, and eventually onto the porch. This was the first step. Then they were allowed to go further onto the pathway and the lawn. It was an amazing experience to see them as they explored, moving the small pebbles around and sniffing the small plants. If a bird sang out or there was a strange noise, Kitty immediately called them back, and they responded and went back inside. As they got bigger they became braver, until the various sounds didn't worry them as much. Eventually they became independent, and began to play games.

Cleo and Tiga near one of their favourite places, the small pond.

Conrad sits near the small pond.

Conrad was the most alert of the three kittens. He was also the first to vanish if something or someone arrived at the house. He was a fast runner, as were the others, and loved to race across the lawn and climb a tree in lightning speed. Although he was the largest cat and started to outgrow the others, including Kitty, he was always gentle and respectful towards them.

Of course at meal times he got his share of the food, and generally was the first to have some seconds from the other cat's plates if they decided to leave before they had finished. As a male cat, he would eventually run into another male. This could be tricky, as the wild male cats are particularly territorial. Kitty brought a big male Tabby once when they were young. Later on, some other cats came round at night, and one night Conrad got into a fight. Apparently he stood up to the other cat, which went away. There was a great uproar which woke me up, but I only saw two eyes disappearing into the dark night.

Cats are very observant and will always take an interest in what is going on around their house. Because we had a large property they seldom went roaming off too far, and kept away from the road as well. This was good because there was some thick bush near the river inhabited by some fairly large Goannas.

Once we ordered a pile of sand. The cats went over to explore it and see what it was. Mum also built a Terracotta bird bath, and this was also of interest to the cats. Anything new seemed interesting to them. If we left the car out at night, by the morning there were lots of little paw marks on the roof and the bonnet. We were always wary of backing or moving off from in front of the house, and checked to make sure no one was sitting under the car.

Left to Right - Kitty and Tiga look at the sand, while Cleo checks out the bird bath.

The cats liked to find different places to rest during the day and at night. Cleo slept behind the radio in my room, while Conrad was often on top of the refrigerator. Kitty liked to sleep on the video player, while Tiga was on the top edge of a chair, or on Mum's bed. Sometimes they would be somewhere else, you never knew where they would turn up, even in a basin in the wash tub.

Tiga was well camouflaged and almost invisible when she sat on the carpet, so we had to watch where we walked. Everyone had their own spot in the house. Kitty and Tiga got along well, and would often share a place, while Cleo and Conrad were more independent. However they all got along well with each other which was a relief. The local pound in Mareeba had a lot of cats in it, and it was often difficult to find homes for them. We had the time to look after them, so we decided to keep them together.

During the day if the weather was good I would collect a lot of leaves. The coconut trees which were growing beside our driveway dropped, among other things, large fronds which we often used as ground cover on the garden. We also collected the coconuts and ate some, while the rest we put on a bonfire. When the pile was big enough I would burn it so we didn't end up with huge piles of unused material. The cats would come and sit on the driveway and watch from a distance. We were always careful to put the fire out. There are often bush fires in Queensland which damage a lot of land. Most of the trees are specially adapted to survive these events. Even the Termite mounds are able to survive. We had a few fires near our property, but they were mostly just burn-offs which people do themselves.

We also made a campfire near our house. It was fun to sit outside, at least when there weren't too many mosquitoes. We lived in an area which was known for Dengue fever. Ironically I had already had this, when we lived in Fiji. I also had caught Malaria in Papua New Guinea, so we invested in mosquito coils and some long-sleeved clothes as well. The cats only had to worry about the ticks, and of course fleas which were often carried by the local wildlife, particularly the various Marsupial mammals.

Kitty was the most adventurous of the group, at least as far as going for longer trips was concerned. Now and then she would disappear for a while, maybe even a couple of days, and then come back again. It was hard to tell where she went - our property was over 40 hectares in size, and mostly covered in bush, and the neighbouring property also had bush and there was a National Park nearby as well. So basically there was miles of open areas to explore. We used to worry a bit, thinking about the wild animals out there, but in the end it was Kitty's choice to go "walkabout" so to speak. The others were less keen, and only Cleo and Conrad would sometimes follow me when I went out with a torch at night.

Some of the animals which came out at night included : Above left - the Bandicoot, above right - a Papuan Frogmouth. On the right Kitty is practising her climbing on the Jacaranda tree. Our cats have very little fear of heights, and loved to climb various trees as well as other structures. They could jump from branch to branch on the trees and would often play games of tag around the garden. They also enjoyed a game which was like hide and seek around the base of the palm trees. They had the occasional dust bath, and then spent hours cleaning themselves.

After the rainy season as we approached the Autumn, the weather became drier. The early morning mist settled on the grass, and a cold air stream could be felt in the evening. The cats noticed the change too, and seemed to become excited and more energetic, especially in the morning. Before we had breakfast they would rush around and play games, hopping from one chair to another, or scampering around the room. They generally stopped to eat and we also gave them a saucer of milk. Depending on how they felt, they would then either go outside or just have a sleep.

It was good to have a routine, and the cats also adapted to this quite easily. Sometimes one would arrive earlier than usual looking for food, or maybe later. There weren,t many complaints, but it was a bit difficult with Tiga who was a big fusspot about her food. She refused to eat the same meat as the other cats, who occasionally looked at her in surprise. She would only eat fresh pieces of chicken, and also she would SOMETIMES eat fresh fish, or a bit of Tuna flakes, and nothing else apart from the dry food and milk!

Tiga's unusual eating habit soon caused issues with the other cats. They noticed that she was getting something different, so naturally became interested. Conrad came over to try some of the chicken, then Cleo and even Kitty. Soon Tiga was surrounded and would leave her plate to the other cats. I had to stop this kind of behaviour. We tried giving the other cats a bit of chicken as well, and this seemed to work. At least Tiga had some time to chew through her meals before someone else came along. Eventually we fed her earlier, or when the others weren't around. If they tried to take her food we just picked them up and put them back at their own plate. Tiga was always the quietest cat, and rarely got angry.

Being the largest cat, Conrad also ate the most. He often finished his food first, and then moved on to another plate. Cleo didn't mind sharing, but Kitty and Tiga weren,t so impressed. We then gave Conrad a bigger helping of cat food so that he ate longer than the others. This seemed to solve the problem, and everyone was happy again.

Fun and games - Conrad and Cleo play in the garden.

Outside there was time to run around, get fit and learn about life. The kittens made up games like hide and seek, and Kitty would join in the fun. It was good to have several cats, and they would play together as a group for hours. If it started to rain everyone came in to the porch and licked themselves, and waited for the rain to stop before going out again.

In the evening as the sun set again, the cats would come inside for a meal. Then they might go out and sit on the lawn, and watch the night fall.

6. Water is life.

As Christians we might say that "Jesus is life", yet there is also no doubt that, at least in this world, we all need water to survive. People, animals and plants, all the same. For a drink we need clean water, and it has to be a regular supply. The cats also drink and we gave them a bowl inside the house which was always filled. Outside they could also drink from the small pond, as did our chickens and Guinea fowls.

It is hard to describe the problems which many people have in the outback concerning water. Many houses near us had several types of water systems, from rivers and dams to bores and rainwater. There was a long drought before we came to our farm, and now and then we had a feeling what it was like. Although we were nearer to water than a lot of other places, we could still have months with no rain at all. The ground would become hard, the grass would dry up, and trees would struggle and stop growing. There was dust, and even small whirlwinds which we called "dust devils". We had to water the garden a lot or it would dry up and keep the water containers filled for the animals.

The dry weather also brought with it the fire season. There was a Volunteer Fire Brigade which was always ready to help people in an emergency. We had some fires near us, but not on our property. There had been fires in the past, and some charred tree trunks still remained in the bush. Most of the trees are adapted to survive the fires, and even the Termite mounds survive them. Most animals run for cover if a fire starts, and afterwards the forest re-generates quickly back.

People also have controlled burn-offs to reduce the amount of "fuel" or material in the bush which can burn. They make a fire break, and then light certain areas and burn them. Fire trucks keep an eye on the flames to make sure they don't move too far. Permission is sought before anyone else can conduct a burn-off, and the best times are after some rain and when it isn't windy. When the rains return, the fire season is over, and we may get heavy rain and floods. Sometimes roads are washed out and people are cut off for several days or longer.

In the dry parts of the Tablelands we relied on various ways to get water. Mostly there were dams, bores, river pumps and rainwater. The rainwater came quite regularly, except during the dry season when we had to pump water from the river. Generally the river water was quite clean although we never drank it, as it wasn't that clean. Likewise we always boiled the rainwater as well, or otherwise we just bought some springwater in bottles.

The cats enjoyed climbing up the ladders onto the two water tanks, and would either have a rest up there or sit and watch things. Cleo in particular liked this, and she also chased the hose when I was watering the garden. Strangely enough, they didn't mind getting a bit wet when it rained, although they weren't so keen to stay outside when it was colder in the winter. We only pumped water in when the river was clear, otherwise we relied on the rainwater. We had large tanks and they could hold plenty of water, so we never ran out.

We sometimes took our dog for a swim in the river, or just sat there and watched it. Wild Ducks, Kingfishers, Herons and Flying Foxes could be seen down there, and also Fishing Eagles. In the river there were Turtles, Prawns, Water snakes, Water Dragons and many kinds of fish and frogs.

A view of the river near our house.

7. The Rural Life.

Living out in the country has some advantages, as well as some problems. If you want to keep more than a few animals around the house, then you definitely have an advantage in the country.

Our property was at least half an hour's drive from the main town Mareeba, and about an hour or so to Cairns on the coast, or to Lake Tinaroo and Atherton the other way. We had a rough dirt road at the end of the paved section, and a long driveway lined with coconut trees. The grass was long near the house, and we got a tractor to cut the longer grass back, and the rest we cut ourselves. It took several years to get the grass back to the fenceline, and we also had many holes which were dug out by Kangaroos and Pigs to fill in before we could mow it. We then got some new holes dug by the Kangaroos, so we tried to strengthen the fences. This was hardly much use, as the Roos simply jumped over them. Anyway, we tried to shoo them off the lawns, and we eventually had a reasonable open area around the house.

The cats also liked to play on the lawn. They would often run at high speeds across to a post or a gate, and hurtle up to the top. Cleo was an expert at climbing posts, and had amazing balance to stand on the top.

When is the washing going to be done?

Another good reason to have a short lawn was because of the snakes. They liked the long grass, but didn't like moving across the open ground as much. We had some fenced paddocks and an old boundary fence which was broken in many places. My sister kept some Horses in the paddocks which had barbed and electric wire around them, but the old boundary fence on our property was useless. The years of being hammered by wild pigs, wild horses and wild cattle had taken it's toll. Add to that the Kangaroos and Wallabies, and the fence had collapsed. It seemed futile to even think about repairing it.

There was one main track through the bush along which you could walk across the property as far as another boundary. A dam had been built, but it had been broken by the water pressure and collapsed. It was a long way from our house anyway, and we only used the tracks for walking and some bicycle riding. I made another track from one of the paddocks near our house, and maintained one along the fenceline until it became quite damp, so I left it alone. There was also a small wetlands near some bush which was mainly used by frogs in the wet season. They laid their eggs there, and the tadpoles stayed there until they left the water as small frogs.

Some frogs from around the place -
Below - White-lipped tree frog,
Right top - Barred frogs,
Right below - Rocket frog.

Morning dew covers the fields.

The cats rarely ventured far from our house, although now and then we heard that one had been seen as far as our entrance, which was only about four or five hundred metres from the house. Kitty was more adventurous, and occasionally disappeared for a couple of days. We didn't encourage them to travel, as there was an element of danger, particularly in the bush. Mostly the cats just relaxed around the house, passing the time of day sitting in the sun early on, and then moving into the shade when it got hotter in the afternoon. They didn't mind where they sat, but they often preferred to be high up, on a table or a chair or a couch etc.

By the time the kittens had reached a year old, they were becoming more independent. At a year and a half they were more confident about where they belonged, and they knew that the house was their own. Kitty was still a bit restless, as always, but when the kittens settled down she also felt the same. There was time to explore, a time to rest and a time to eat. The cats didn't always keep to the same time, and began to show their individual preferences more often, especially when it came to food. After all, they were all individuals as well as a family.

I should also not forget to mention our dog. Leo was only eight weeks old when he came to stay with us. There was a litter of six puppies near the Clohesy River, down Koah Road, and the owners had a dog which was rescued from the Mareeba Animal Rescue centre. It had the puppies, and the owners wanted them to be rehomed. We got a light-brown coloured male puppy, and his coat reminded us of the lions which we had seen in Africa. He blended in with the dry landscape around us, so we called him Leo.

Leo is a good watchdog, and loves swimming in the river and in our creek. It was always good to cool off after a long walk from one end of our farm to the next, where the creek flowed in the bush. We taught him to be wary of snakes, and he learned early on to avoid them. He liked playing with the other dogs, and running through the long grass.

We took Leo for walks every day, which was important for an active "working-type" dog, so to speak. Having kept dogs for over thirty years we understood how valuable it is for them to have excercise. Even so, he still managed to go for a roam or "walk-about" on his own from time to time - even forty acres wasn't big enough for him!

It was rare for Wild horses, or Brumbies to come onto the property, however this happened several times. They were known around the Koah area, and most people just left them alone. Most were descended from horses which escaped into the bush, where they survived as best they could. If the grazing was limited, they would travel and come near the settlement to find some fresh grass. Some of them were quite tame, and they occasionally got into trouble with other horses. They were very strong - we once had an iron post kicked and broken in half.

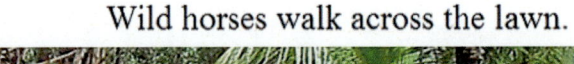

Wild horses walk across the lawn.

A group of Brumbies near a fence at Koah.

8. The Mysterious Visitor.

One day, a large Monitor Lizard came plodding up the driveway. They were fairly common in the forest near the river, but rarely came up our way. The cat's reaction was amazing ; they rushed to the door and stood there, almost petrified. Goannas are big and are known to hunt small animals. The lizard looked at our house, and then started to walk around past the dog kennel. Leo was not impressed. A loud bark was heard from the run, and the lizard jumped sideways. It then tried to climb a small palm tree, but it was only about eight feet tall. I hung a net over its head, and it came down and headed off back down the driveway until it came to a coconut tree. It climbed the tree, stayed up there for a while, and eventually disappeared.

We liked having Geckos at the farm, and they could often be seen in the house. They were useful for catching some insects such as cockroaches and mosquitoes. We were constantly telling our cats to leave them alone!

Geckos are not so scary.

Another visitor to our property was the Frilled Lizard. They usually turned up just at the beginning of the dry summer time. The smaller juveniles stayed out in the bush, while the adults came and explored the lawn. If you approached them, they would walk away and climb a tree, and then they would just sit there, as if they thought they were invisible. They didn't bother anything, although the chooks with babies were a bit wary of them, as well as the Guinea fowls, but the cats basically just ignored them once they realised that they were just visiting.

Left : A Frilled Lizard sits on a Lychee tree at the farm.

The smaller birds such as Honeyeaters had to be more careful, particularly during the nesting season. Lizards are good at finding things to eat, and are versatile predators. Some of the bigger lizards seemed to be territorial, and stayed near the same places for several weeks. As the weather changed, they gradually moved on back to the bush again. Then we rarely saw them again until the next year.

Some of the other lizards we saw included Water Dragons and Skinks. The Water Dragons lived mainly by the river and along the sides of the creeks. They sat on the branches of trees overlooking the water, and when disturbed they would jump in and swim away. The skinks would move about in the sun, and sometimes stop on a rock or a log. They also climbed trees, and were always on the move. Most of the reptiles laid eggs in various places, such as under logs or stones. There were also freshwater turtles in the river and the streams.

9. Sitting by a Pond.

At first we thought we might use our pool as a dam. Indeed we often needed some extra water if there was a power cut (which is common in our area.) Then we thought that we might use it as a fish pond. It was mainly filled with rainwater, so we put a few plants in, lots of fish and some prawns. The pond was popular with the local wildlife, who used to come for a drink or a swim. Frogs liked to hide in the Palm trees which surrounded it, and made a great chorus in the rain. Snakes would follow the frogs, and we even had some Water snakes having a swim in it. Frogs and Toads also visited regularly, and various birds would stop by for a wash and to drink from the birdbath. We even had two wild ducks which came for a swim.

The cats weren't concerned much with the visitors around the pond. They also never tried to catch our fish, which was a relief. There was a bigger threat to them from the wildlife - Kingfishers and Kookaburras in particular would come and have a snoop around, but usually they just moved on. The water was quite clean and was often refreshed by the rain which was generally cleaner than the river water.

In the dam we had several kinds of fish. Many of them had a real population which reproduced with lots of small fry. We had Eastern Rainbowfish, Empire Gudgeons, Platies, Goldfish, Silver Sharks and also a Black Shark who was the biggest fish. They liked coming up for a slice of bread, and we also gave them fish food.

Some fish like the Sharks and Goldfish eat algae and plants, so they could feed themselves easily. Others caught insects on the surface and also ate mosquito larvae. Sometimes we had Dragonflies, Damselflies and Water beetles which came to the pond. We had some wetlands as well as a small creek and this supported many other creatures. There were fish, freshwater Crayfish or "Yabbies", various insects and even Water rats. The creek dried up in the summer, leaving only a few permanent pools out in the forest.

In contrast the main river had a good flow most of the year. There were plenty of fish and amphibians in it, and different types of water birds and reptiles could also be seen there.

Top right : A Lotus flower.
Below left : A Black Shark.
Below right : A Rainbowfish.

A view of the creek near our house.

Along with the lizards called Water Dragons, there were also some sightings of the Platypus in some of the streams, although not in our stream which was often dried out for part of the year. Many tracks could be seen along the stream bed, as the animals searched for water.
We used to practice identifying what they belonged to - a wallaby, a dog, a pig, a snake or whatever. I spent some time rescuing stranded animals such as tadpoles, fish and small crabs which were stuck in the drying-up pools, and released them near some permanent water. The track near our house took us across the creek, and on to the boundary with a neighbour's property.

While the dry weather made life difficult for some animals, it didn't bother the turtles - they just got up and walked away to another place!

A Freshwater Turtle.

A Redclaw crayfish or "Yabby".

Most of the streams around us eventually drained into the main river, or into one of the many lakes which are on the Atherton Tablelands. The largest lake was called Lake Tinaroo, which was built as a dam and is used for irrigation as well as recreation.

While working on a building site I learned a bit about local history - stories about the early days, the gold prospecting, explorers, farmers and so on. Most places had invested in dams, which were always valuable for isolated communities. There was a lot of talk about how to construct them, and also what to avoid. We worked on a traditional stone wall, breaking the pieces to a certain size, and placing them in the wall, without any concrete. It was hard work but fun too. There was a large dam which looked like a lake next to the building site, and it had some Water lillies and Bullrushes growing around the sides. There were fish and eels in the water, and water birds stopped by as well.

10. The Great Serpent.

Some people like snakes, and some don't. We have lots of snakes on the Tablelands. Some are harmless, others not so. But either way, they are part of the environment. Many of them hunt small marsupials such as mice and rats, while others hunt birds, bats and so on. We noticed that our chooks always made a point of nesting way out on the limbs of the Mango tree at night. Perhaps they were aware of the danger posed by the snakes, in particular the Pythons.

The Amethystine Python is known to grow to five metres long, and is the longest snake in the world. It feeds on a wide range of animals, including poultry. Even birds in chicken runs are not always safe, and we heard plenty of stories about the exploites of the Pythons. The first snake which was seen by our cats was a small python which was on our front porch. They were wary of getting too close to it, which was good, and we encouraged them to be vigilant around snakes in general and tried to discourage them from getting too close.

Cleo observes a Northern Tree snake which has climbed down from a palm tree.

There were many different kinds of snakes on the Tablelands. Some like the King Brown, Papuan Whip snake and Taipan were venomous, while others like the Freshwater snake, Pythons and Tree snakes were not venomous. Snakes are useful as they often hunt rats, which can eat a lot of fruit and crops if the population increases too much. We often saw snakes hunting in the pastures or near piles of hay, where the mice had been making nests. Sometimes the Pythons would follow the mice into the chook runs where they had dug in to look for seed.

A Carpet Python.   A Brown Tree Snake.

Fortunately cats are fast and alert, as well as agile to escape from a snake. Because of this they will rarely become a target for most snakes. Snakes will hunt smaller animals, such as lizards or birds. Most of the snakes lived out in the bush, and we rarely saw them during the daytime. At night some kinds would come out to explore, and would come across the lawn under the cover of darkness.

During the day we would see some snakes sitting out in the sun to catch the warmth. You had to be careful when you went for a walk as they could sometimes sit under the long grass by a pathway. The Tree snakes were hard to find during the day, as they often stayed high up on the trees, and were well hidden. The ground snakes would hide under logs or in holes and crevices at the base of trees, and so on. We were told to be careful when lifting tarpaulins, particularly in the winter as some snakes liked to hide underneath them. Snakes can easily swim across rivers, and some kinds actually live in them. Some kinds will lay eggs, while others have live offspring. I sometimes found snake skins near our house, and on the roof was not unusual.

A scene from the bush with a Termite mound.

11. Life around the house.

A meeting on the porch.

Our house was a typical concrete block farmhouse. It was cool in the summer, and there was a breeze which came across the fields. There was plenty of room, except there weren't many cupboards in the house. This meant a lack of storage space. There was room on the verandas, so some things were stored there. You could say most of the junk ended up on the porch.

The cats liked climbing and exploring. They had found a way to get up onto the roof, and the garage, and the small shed, and so on. Even after about three years, they were still quite shy, and usually ran away when people came to visit. They were always exploring, and anything new was inspected with great interest. I built a small kennel for our dog, and it was full of cats before our dog ever got to see it. The doghouse was made of wood and was placed in the run, and while I was building it the cats would jump around on top of it, playing games and having a great time. A lot of time was spent like this, and they would bring various things onto the porch, such as pieces of wood or leaves to play with. Later in the day they would come in and sit in the kitchen looking at the fridge, or waiting around until they got their meals. There wasn't much conflict at mealtime. We made sure that everyone got something, and tried to put the plates out at the same time. If you put one at a time, no one was sure whose plate it was, and this resulted in a bit of a mess, with everyone going for the same plate. We then had to separate them and direct each cat to it's own plate. Only Tiga was fed separately because she refused to eat the regular cat food, which was mostly Kangaroo meat. The other cats would also show an interest in Tiga's food, and we had to keep an eye on things. But usually there weren't any real problems. There were a few "play fights" in the kitchen, and only once did a cat hiss at another one while eating. Mostly they just shared what they had when they had finished eating. After three years this situation was still the same, and we were happy too.

Depending on the weather, the cats would spend the morning inside or outside, watching things or just relaxing. Our free-range chickens and Guinea fowls took little interest in them, and a local Peacock was the same. The Wallabies sometimes watched, but also ignored them. Only the birds would kick up a fuss, especially the Honeyeaters. They would appear suddenly in a group, squawking loudly at a cat. Our cats were amused at this, and also curious about the noise. The birds seemed to know that the cats were a threat in some way. Cats are carnivores, so it was inevitable that this would happen. Anyway, we kept our cats well fed and encouraged them not to set the birds. Generally this worked, and the birds stayed away from the cats anyway. At night it was more difficult to keep track of what was going on. We sometimes had Frogmouths and even Owls coming in to hunt. The chickens were wary of the Owls, and if one sat in the Mango tree, they would let out a low sound which was almost like a kind of howl. This was a warning signal, and we always knew that something was out there.

Generally there wasn't much going on during the day. The Magpie Larks would roam across the lawn collecting insects, and other birds such as the Spur-winged Plover and the Sacred Ibis often came to find some food. Occasionally there was an arguement with the Guinea fowls who were a bit more protective of their turf. Most of the birds ate seeds or small insects, and there was usually plenty for them to find in the spring and summer, but not so much in the colder weather. In the winter the birds only came now and then, while the Guinea fowl would travel further to find insects and other things.

The dry season was interesting, but also hard on the land. The plants and trees stopped growing, the grass dried up and leaves fell from the trees. There was also a lot of dust, Our soil was loam and clay, and it broke up easily. The birds often had dust baths, while our cats also rolled in the dust. I put some sand around to keep the weeds down, and of course this was popular with the cats too. The lawn changed colour from green to brown. When it was long, I would mow it and the chooks would follow the mower around, waiting for insects to fly up, but now there was no need to mow it. Large grasshoppers flew in from time to time, and Rhinoceros beetles could also be seen. The grasshoppers and locusts would eat any leaves they could find, and caterpillars would also munch away on various crops that we planted.

A dry spell : Conrad and Tiga sit on the lawn, watching the world go by...

12. The Forest beyond.

Grass trees growing in our bush may be over 500 years old.

The forest around our property was dry woodlands, typical of the rugged outback environment in Australia. There were a few patches of rainforest plants, mostly adjacent to the streams and creeks, as well as a large plantation of Eucalyptus trees which were supposed to be a commercial venture. Huge termite mounds could be seen in various places, and the old hollow trunks of trees gave refuge to many creatures. There were Oppossums, Bandicoots, Echidnas, Squirrel Gliders, Potaroos and other marsupials, as well as many reptiles and bats. The small wetlands supported several species of frogs, and there were local Yabbies (crayfish) in the stream which dug deep holes to survive through the dry period. There were also some rare animals such as the Northern Quoll. Some of the bats are also quite rare, and are known from around Mareeba.

The fruit bats often came out of the forest at night, and gathered around our palm trees to eat the seeds. You knew where they were nesting because of the noise they made. It was no different when they found the seeds - there was a great racket as the bats tried to get the

the best position on the tree. In the dry season the bats would also try and eat the immature fruit of the coconut trees, and would often spend hours sitting up there. Squirrel gliders would also use the coconut trees as a nesting site - we used to spot them with a torch on the trunks at night. Most of the bats were insect eaters, and some of them roosted in the banana plantation, hanging under the dry leaves during the day and flying among the trees at night.

The fruit bats, by reputation, were often considered to be a bit of a nuisance, because they often ate fruit which had been planted for people. The worst time for us was during the Mango season, when the big mango trees were laden with fruit. Dozens of fruit bats would arrive and hoe in to the mangoes, dropping them on the ground, sometimes hundreds of meters away from the tree. Our chooks who nested in the tree were also frustrated, and sometimes flew out and went somewhere else for the night. The noise was tremendous as the bats argued over the mangoes. In the morning I went out and raked up all the fallen fruit and leaves.

Other kinds of fruits were also popular with the Flying foxes. We often see them hovering over the banana plantation. The bananas are covered in bags which are tied on at the top. However the bats are smart, and so they force their way in and eat the bananas at the top of the bunch. The first time I saw this happen, I went out and tapped the

Mangoes are popular with bats...

side of the bag. A bat poked it's head out with a banana in it's mouth, and looked at me as if to say "what are you doing here?" Then it flew off with the banana! Anyway, we just had to put up with animals on the property. As long as they kept out of our house, and didn't go after our domestic animals, and didn't wreck too many things and eat all our crops, we don't really mind them. Well, sort of like that, maybe in a perfect world!

A Mango tree in bloom. It will soon put out some fruit.

At one point the bats also began to roost in the tree during the day. Then they could just climb around and chew whatever fruit they wanted. Strangely enough, one of our cats noticed this. Cleo was always very alert and would notice if something was different. She was used to sitting on top of the water tanks, which were only a few meters away from the Mango trees. If a bat dropped a mango, it would often crash onto the tank. Cleo stalked towards the tree, and just sat there, looking at it. The bats were high up and stayed there most of the day, until the evening when they dispersed out to look for food. She never went near them, but knew where they were.

Both the Black Flying-fox and the Spectacled Flying-foxes, which can have wingspans of over a meter wide, were regular visitors on our farm. We also saw the Little Red Flying-fox, and the Blossom bat which looks like a small flying-fox. I rescued a baby flying-fox which had been abandoned by it's parent, and gave it to the local "bat rescue" group, who help bats. The bats often roosted in colonies on the Tablelands, and once we saw hundreds in the big trees by the river. They flew away over our house in the evening like a cloud.

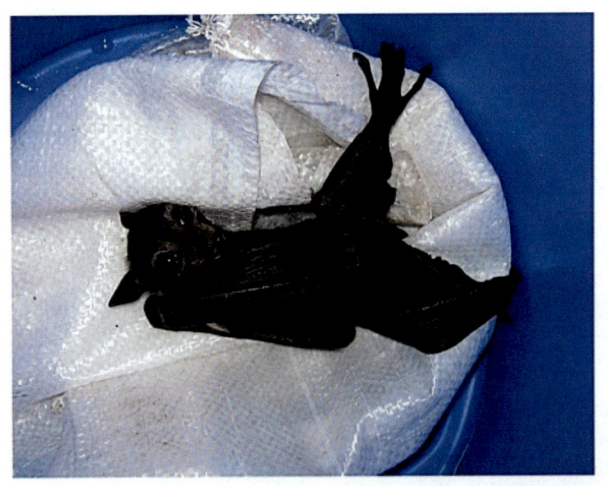

This small bat was rescued at our property, and given to the local bat rescue group.

Sometimes we were faced with unforeseen problems. A small bat being abandoned, another caught in a fence, and so on. We always took some time out to try and help a bit and it was easy to make a bit of an effort now and then. We liked to be in the country, and to see the wildlife, but we also respected the fact that people must farm the land. Wildlife and farming don't always mix too well. And there were plenty of examples which were shared with us from the local people too.

We sometimes caught a snake trying to munch one of our chickens. People told us the best thing to do was to relocate them far away from the property. I had learned how to catch snakes when I was living in Africa, so I tried this, and it was successful. We relocated several snakes and they didn't return to our place. Otherwise they will always find their way back again.

Right : A Flying Fox checks out the fruit on a Golden Palm tree.

13. The Rain Time.

    After Christmas and in January in the new year we would begin to get some rain. It was also called the "cyclone season", after the big tropical storms which are known to hit the coast of Queensland. The cyclones brought high winds, torrential rain and flooding to anywhere they made landfall. Roads were blocked, bridges washed out and the rivers would flood too. Fortunately we lived further inland away from the coast, and we tended not to experience the full force of the winds. Power cuts were likely, and the bridge further down the road was often flooded. We just had to wait for the storm to pass by.

The Barron river in flood.

The flooded bridge.

During a storm, not surprisingly, our cats would stay inside. But then they would go out again, and explore. Cleo was usually the first to go looking around. She explored the fallen branches, leaves, coconuts and so on. Even if it was still wet or there was drizzle, she would still be out there. Tiga was usually not far behind, sitting near the house watching, and occasionally Conrad and Kitty would venture out too.

The rain left big puddles of water around the house. At night the sound of crickets and frogs could be heard. The frogs sometimes started croaking just before a storm, or when it was going to rain. They made a lot of noise, with different chirps and calls. Their singing could go on through the night, until the early hours of the next day.

The rain would also drive other animals out of their hiding places. Sometimes snakes would come, especially the water snakes, and have a swim in our pond. The toads would also be hopping around, and at night they waited by the lights for something to eat. The toads were introduced to Australia to help eat insects which damaged the sugar cane plantations, but they don't seem to have gotten many thanks for it. The Geckos also ate some bugs, and the winged termites would sometimes arrive in the hundreds after some heavy rain.

The Amphibian's Orchestra :
Below and top right - Tree frogs,
below right - Cane toad.

Our dog Leo was always ready for a swim across the river. After the storms there were always some neat sunsets in the evening. As the saying goes, "Every cloud has a silver lining", which to me was a renewal of the land, a cleansing of the streams, and at least a chance to grow a few crops without irrigating all the time. And of course, water is fun too!

14. The Winter comes...

When we talk about the winter in Northern Queensland, some people really think we are just joking. Compared to colder countries, such as New Zealand where we used to live, it would sound like the summer, not the winter. Yet we do have cold weather, as well as big changes in temperature from day to night. A morning frost is not uncommon, and sometimes we hear about hail falling in other parts of the state.

The animals notice the difference too. Our cats and the dog look for the sun in the morning, and like sitting outside late in the afternoon to catch the warm rays. The Kangaroos find less to eat in the bush, so they spend more time digging around our lawn. Different birds appear, they probably live higher up in the cool mountain areas most of the year, but come down as the weather gets cooler. The water in the river cools off, so we don't swim as much. For about three months the weather is cool, and we like to make fires and sit outside.

Cleo sits in the shade on a sunny winter day.

We had several aquariums, some of which needed heaters for a few months in the cold weather. The breeze from across the Tablelands was also cold at times, and it was good to have a pullover handy. We collected firewood and piled it up, and the dry leaves and twigs made it easy to start a fire. During the dry season there were often burnoffs done by the volunteer fire service. We always had permission to light small fires any time of the year.

If the winter was dry, we pumped a lot of water into our tanks to irrigate the garden, provide water for the animals and so on. My job was to keep the opening on the pipe clear in the river, and start the pump. Sometimes there was debris from flooding, and when the wet season came I usually had to move the pump to higher ground, away from the flooded river. Sometimes people lost their pumps, as the rivers could come up very fast.

Above left - Kitty sits by one of the fish tanks.
Left - A local Gudgeon.
Above - Tiga sits on top of an aquarium.

Gradually, as the temperatures got colder, the cats would spend more time inside rather than out, especially in the evenings. In the wild a cat would find shelter in trees, or in hollow logs, to escape the cold. The streams dried out, and the wild animals began to travel from the bush towards the permanent water holes and the main river. In some places there were signs of digging by wild pigs, who liked to wade across the streams and explore the muddy regions. Cattle would also come down to the river, as if to camp there, and forage in the vegetation, and sometimes wild horses came as well. The dry weather meant that there was less grazing for animals such as Kangaroos and Wallabies, so they also began to migrate around the Tablelands.

The bats weren't affected in any way much. They still came out in the evening, some searching for insects, others still looking for fruit. The fish and the birds weren't quite as active, and the reptiles generally hibernated at this time of year. During the full moons the light shone through the trees and later there was a thick mist like a fog which descended across the land.

15. Conrad goes exploring.

Like most animals, as well as people, cats are interested in their surroundings. At first they only travel short distances. In our case, they were particularly cautious. They realised that there were lots of other "things" out there, and they weren't all friendly either.

Kitty was watchful from the beginning. She may have taught her kittens a bit, or they just learned as they grew up. As they grew they explore the corners of our lawn, which was surrounded by two or three foot high grass. There were small tracks going through the paddocks made by the Kangaroos, and other animals. The cats could also make use of these tracks. Once I saw a wild cat in a field. It's eyes lit up in the torchlight, and it sat and stared across towards me. Our cats played outside on the lawn in the evening, and gradually got to know the environment around them, and their territory.

At first they were curious about everything going on. They would follow us to the garden, then to the compost, and then to the clothesline to see the washing go out. Gradually they became used to seeing the daily chores and lost interest in them. Cleo was usually the most enthusiastic, and liked running across the lawn to climb something. Conrad was a bit cautious, and would sit and wait before following anyone. However, one night Conrad didn't come back for breakfast. We waited all day, and by the evening he still hadn't returned.

We were a bit worried, although we knew that Kitty and Cleo had both been out overnight too. Kitty would often stay out, but she always came back again. We called our neighbour once, but no one knew where they went. The next day, there was still no sign of Conrad. I had a look down near the river, and called out, but there was no sign of him. No worries, I thought, he'll be back sometime. The other cats seemed to realise that he was missing. They were a close-knit group in some ways. They liked to have their own space, but also enjoyed each other's company from time to time. But where was Conrad?

At about 3.00 am there was a "meeow" at the door. I looked outside, and sure enough there was Conrad. We were glad to see him back. We don't know exactly why the cats disappear from time to time. Maybe they just like to explore, and go walkabout. Anyway, he got a meal and decided to stay inside.

Because our house had no cat door, we usually had to open a door for the cats to come in. They would sit and meeow, and even move from door to door. If we left a door open, there was always a risk that something else might come in, such as a chicken, or maybe a snake. It wasn't the best situation to have, particularly with four cats. Hopefully we will eventually get at least one cat door installed.

We extended the lawn area around the house, with some help from a local farmer who had a tractor and a slasher, and I used a brushcutter to make the area even wider. This was important, mainly because of the snakes which liked to move through the longer grass. For the cats, it meant that they had more open space to explore. I developed a field to plant some more crops, and put a fence in to try and discourage the Kangaroos. You can never stop the Kangaroos, they just jump over almost anything, but at least it can put them off from simply walking through your vegetables. Even if they don't eat them, they can trample the new seedlings.

The cats didn't mind the fences. At first they looked for small holes along the sides, and then they started climbing over them. Eventually it became fun, and they would run towards a fence and almost fly over it, or climb a post before jumping off the other side. There was time to explore the vegetables, the watermelons, rockmelons, pumpkins and so on. Chasing grasshoppers became a big occupation. At least they kept some of them away from eating the plants. Growing melons and other crops is always a problem if there are mice or rats around. Even the seeds can be accidently dug up and eaten by something. I often spent time replanting seeds which got lost. Cleo would come out and watch, always interested in something new. Sometimes she got in the way as well, and liked to dig holes where I had planted something.

Cleo and Conrad got along well with each other. They were usually the first ones to run out or climb a tree, and Kitty and Tiga were not far behind. They rarely had arguements, which was a relief, and they even shared their food with each other.

Kitty would sometimes take the lead. As she was the senior cat of the group (as well as their Mum) this was quite normal. Kitty was very strong, and had amazing balance for climbing and jumping. Conrad was also fast and climbed trees easily. Sometimes they played games, stalking each other like lions, or waiting behind a tree trunk to pounce on another cat. When they were small they played a lot, but as they got bigger, they were less inclined to play, and became more settled and laid back about life. Before they would run and play tackle on the lawn, and also have wrestling matches. Now, they spent more time relaxing in the shade, just looking out across the grass. But now and then, there was an outburst of energy, and the games started once again. Who could climb the fastest, who could reach a new branch on a tree, a game of tag, and so on. And of course, there were also those trips into the dark...

16. Climbing high.

Cats are well known for their agility. It is part of their life, to be able to survive or adapt to a particular environment. When a cat is living in a house, it is not as important to be able to climb a tree, or scamper over a fence to escape something. But the cats don't lose their ability to be strong and fast. They may not be Lions, or Jaguars, or other big cats, but nonetheless they still share some of the same abilities that their wild cousins have.

We watched our cats as they explored the garden. Following each other was always obvious to see, and one or another would take the lead depending on what was going on. Hide and seek was popular, and also to find a new part of the plantation or the garden. There was always something to do on the farm. The cats stayed away from the horses, as they were big to them, but they watched them gallop past. We had a gazebo as a car port, with a tarpaulin as the roof, and this was a good spot to sit and watch the world go by.

Cleo practises climbing some of the trees.

A White-breasted Sea-Eagle flies near the river. It may have a wingspan of up to two meters wide.

The cats had grown accustomed to seeing various animals around the property. There were plenty of Ibis, Plovers, Magpie Larks and of course the free-range Chickens and the Guinea Fowls. Now and then a bird of prey would appear. Usually it was a small Falcon, or sometimes a larger bird such as a Wedge-tailed Eagle or a Hawk. When such a bird landed in a tree, the Guinea Fowl were the first to sound an alarm along with the Chooks. The Hawks were always on the lookout for small birds and animals, particularly in the spring, summer and early winter too.

If one of them was hungry enough, it would fly down and look for a small Guinea Fowl or a Chicken. They would even crash into the mesh surrounding the chicken run if there were some birds inside, or sit on top of it. There was a tremendous noise from the chooks, who let everyone know that something was wrong. This usually sets our dog off too. Sometimes other birds would follow the Falcons and chase them. But we often lost some of our chicks to them.

More rarely we would see an Owl, always after dark. One night an owl landed in the Mango tree. It just sat there, staring at the chooks, and they made a strange, low sound. They knew that the owl was there even though it was dark. However, the owl wasn't interested in the chickens, it was just looking around, probably going hunting for some small animals in the night.

Cats like to explore at night. At first we were a bit concerned, since there are a number of dangers outside. There were no cars, which was a bonus, but there were certainly plenty of other things. Especially the wild animals, many of which came out to hunt for food at night.

The snakes were always around, but our cats had learned to be wary of them. Dingoes were not as common, nor were wild dogs. Our own dog Leo was a good watchdog, and very alert. He could pick up a smell from some distance away, and his bark was like a big howl which everyone took notice of. The Goannas did not come near our side of the property as much as across the road, near the river where there was more marginal bush and steep gullies. We kept our place tidy, so there was less chance of rats or mice setting up nests. When the small mammals built a nest, this would often attract the snakes, who also had a keen sense of smell.

There were also other animals which were just passing through. The wild pigs generally stayed outside the boundaries and roamed through the bush at night. They lived in groups, and spent most of the time digging around for food, particularly in wet areas. The Echidna or Spiny Anteater was also seen from time to time. They also dug around in ant nests and termite mounds. The Quolls were rarer, but there were plenty of Bandicoots around. Along the creek and the river there were other kinds of Marsupial rodents such as the Giant White-tailed Rat and the Water Rat, and in the bush there were also animals like the Striped Oppossum.

Sometimes we saw another cat. Early on Kitty turned up on the back porch with a large Tabby cat. It sat and watched the kittens who were in the house. Another time a cat which looked like a small lion came to the same door. And once a small striped cat came in the evening and looked around the back of our house. Tiga was there and hissed at it. There were some wild cats in the bush. They survived as best they could, and rarely came near the farms or other houses. We saw a black cat with a white blaze underneath a few times, once near a track on our property, and again lying on the road in the sun. It got up and quickly moved away into the long grass down by the river.

17. Tracks in the Forest.

Above : A forest pool. Inset on the right : The Gudgeon which is found in the creeks and the rivers.

In the period when there was little rain some of the creeks used to almost run dry. There were only a few pools left here and there, and these were often used by wild animals and even domestic stock as watering holes, who would otherwise have to find dams, or travel down to the main river. The smaller rivers such as the Clohesy always had plenty of water, while it was the same in the Barron River. Some animals would walk a long way from out in the bush to reach the river in times of drought. We always remembered to leave plenty of water out for our cats, dog and also the poultry. The chooks began to drink all our dogs water, so I put the container higher up on a block out of their reach.

The cats weren't fussy about where they drank. They usually drank from their bowl in the kitchen, and sometimes they drank from the small pond around the back of our house. When there was heavy rain, the lawn would become flooded and the ground became waterlogged. If there was a Cyclone as well, our water tanks would overflow. Everyone headed for cover and just sat there looking miserable.

Cyclones were particularly scary for the animals. However after a storm they would venture outside again, and inspect the garden. I would be cleaning the place up, collecting the broken branches and sweeping debris off the driveway. Eventually things went back to normal, and the cats got back to their usual routines.

Exploring the garden was always a big deal. Sometimes they would travel further to the banana plantation. At night you could go out with a torch, and a pair of brightly lit eyes could be seen coming towards you in the distance. Or you might hear a "meeow" from behind a fence. I could soon recognise the sound each cat made, like a signal. They all seemed to have their own individual voices.

Cleo explores along the fenceline near a paddock.

18. The Sounds in the Night.

The evening in the winter is often accompanied by a mist, almost like a fog, which descends across the land. Sometimes the visibility is only about ten or so feet, and is unclear beyond that. A torch beam will reveal a shower of tiny drops of water falling like a waterfall.

Regardless, the cats are usually exploring at night, although more recently they have decided to stay at the house after about ten o'clock. Kitty has a spot on the porch on a chair, Conrad sleeps on a large cardboard carton inside, and the other two go where they like. Conrad usually wakes me up at about midnight, scratching on the door to go outside. The others sometimes meeow to come in at about two am.

Occasionally something would disrupt the routine. One night, another cat came and started visiting regularly. It was probably abandoned, and it wasn't popular with our mob. It made a lot of noise, starting at about seven in the evening, and even ignored our dog too. It seemed to be looking for food, and our neighbours had seen it with another large cat down by the river. They were both striped and ginger in color.

Eventually there were some altercations. The new cat was a male, and Conrad stood up and chased it away from the house. Eventually it left altogether and went somewhere else. Peace returned to the property, so to speak. At least our cats could sit on their lawn without being pestered by another cat. I saw a big furry cat once which climbed a post. It looked a bit like an Oppossum, and was probably wild. It jumped down and vanished into the grass.

We had a visit from some domestic cattle, who were looking for water during the dry spell. Fortunately they didn't eat too many of our shrubs, and eventually the owner came on a horse with his dog to collect them. The cats enjoyed camping around outside, sometimes near the house, but often on the driveway. They were well camouflaged at night. Tiga in particular was almost invisible, apart from a small white patch, and the same with Kitty. They would sit and listen to the strange noises at night, the frogs, birds and crickets, and the barking of the dogs in the distance.

Cats on patrol : Kitty, Conrad and Tiga look down the driveway, while Cleo looks back the other way.

There were lots of small lizards around our house, such as the skinks and geckos, as well as bigger types. We liked having them around, and so did the cats...but for other reasons. It was great hunting practice for them, and Kitty had started to teach the others how to hunt. In general they just caught things and let them go. Sometimes things were eaten, so we tried to discourage hunting, and kept everyone well fed. This seemed to work fairly well, and gradually there was less interest in hunting around the house. Keeping the cats well fed seemed to help, but we also needed to tell them off if they started catching geckos, grasshoppers or whatever. It's not easy telling a carnivore not to eat meat, and of course most people like cats to catch mice and rats too....

Cleo practices stalking something.    Tiga and Kitty exploring the lawn.

One of their favourite pastimes is to walk around the fences, peeking into the vegetable gardens and the long grass. Sometimes they would stop and sharpen their claws on a post or a tree trunk, or a piece of wood. We left a few old boards and planks out for this.

Apparently cats need exercise, like most other animals and of course us humans too. Our cats liked to spend a certain amount of time outside too.

Kitty sharpens her claws on a fencepost.

When the weather became dryer the various animals around the place would look for watering places. Our bird bath was popular with frogs and birds, both of which liked to wash or have a drink in it. It was placed in the shade near some palm trees, so that it wouldn't evaporate too fast. The Sunbirds liked to dive in and out, while the frogs would hide in the palm trees.

Conrad watches the world go by as the season changes, and the warm weather sets in.

As the weather becomes warmer, the animals spend more time in the sun, sometimes just sitting around the house in the evening until nightfall when other animals start to appear.

Soon the bats begin their flight across the sky, heading towards a feeding ground somewhere. They come out of the bushland, and are silouetted against the sky. The smaller bats fly in circles, catching insects while others look for nectar from the flowers. Birds like the Large-tailed Nightjar can be heard, and they often land on the grass.

In the daytime the Wagtails play in the garden, flying from tree to tree and sitting on the fences. Smaller birds like Swallowtails also fly across the fields, and the Kookaburras make a loud sound when they have a territorial dispute or something else bothers them. The Ibis are usually the biggest birds around, and they arrive in the late morning and stay for most of the day.

A moth sits on a Ginger leaf during the day like a dry leaf. It will fly away after dark.

Someone had told us about the insects in Queensland. If you planted some crops, the rule was generally "fifty percent for you, and fifty percent for the wildlife." After a couple of years seeing things getting demolished we had to agree that this was true, and it wasn't just the insects that ate things either. Almost everything seemed to want a share. In the summer we liked to plant after the rain, but this coincided with an increase in insects as well.

The Guinea fowl and the chickens helped out a lot. They would walk around the crops, picking bugs and caterpillars off the plants. Frogs, Toads, lizards and ants were also useful like this. Sometimes nature is a best friend as well as a problem.

Top - A Butterfly.
Below left and right - Two beetles.
Bottom left - A Grasshopper.
Bottom right - A Scorpion.

72.

19. The Misty days.

The morning mist hangs across the forest trees.

During the Winter and towards the early Spring we often have a lot of mist. In the evening it comes out of nowhere, settling across the fields and the forest, particularly on a clear night. Sometimes you can see it through the moonlight on a clear night. In the early morning the mist lifts from the ground, leaving a wet dew on the grass and leaves of the trees. On a colder night there may even be a frost.

At this time of the year we may light fires and sit outside, or turn on a heater inside the house. When the weather gets warmer we put the heater away, and just wear pullovers until the Summer. The cats also like to spend more time inside the house, instead of roaming around outside for long periods of time, but they don't mind the colder weather too much and still like to sit on the lawn in the evening.

Mist over the outback.

Going nowhere - Conrad watches the view from the roof of our car.

As the winter wears on the temperatures can drop to as low as 10 C and there is usually a long period of dryer weather. This climate means that the enivironment is favourable for some animals, but not others. Most of the reptiles and some of the marsupials go and hibernate or are not seen as much, while different animals and birds in particular start to visit the farm, such as the birds which normally live higher up in the foothills where the weather is cooler.

When the spring comes there are often showers of rain and eventually more heavy falls. The dry parched ground springs to life with new growth, and many trees begin to flower and bear fruit. We also see an occasional rainbow in the distance.

Conrad and Cleo explore the lawn in the evening.

    The evening was a good time to watch the cats outside. They would wake up from a rest, and have a look around. Most of the day we had a breeze from the North, but in the evening it was calm, and there was always a sunset on the horizon unless it was raining.

    Conrad and Cleo were usually the first to wake up, and Tiga would sometimes be there as well. Kitty liked to sit on the table and observe things. Our Guinea Fowl and Jungle Fowl roamed around the lawn, but didn't take much notice of the cats. Everyone ran for cover if a Hawk flew overhead. We had plenty of dramas with them, and the cats also seemed to realize that they were a threat of some kind. The chickens would generally hide under the plants in the garden, and stay there for a few minutes, while the Roosters would sound an alarm call to warn them about the Hawk. Meanwhile the Guinea Fowl would also make a huge racket, so we always knew when something was there. They would even fly towards a Hawk and try to chase it away, especially when they had their young chicks with them. The chicks would hide in the long grass or under a bush while the parents squawked and ran back and forth towards the other bird. When it flew away they would come out again, but were more watchful than before.

Over the colder months the Kangaroos and Wallabies still roamed across the property. They were frequent visitors in the evening, and often stayed around after dark, digging for roots in the lawn and eating the new shoots of grass. During a full moon you could often see the sillouettes of several Wallabies in a group. They would quickly move away if you approached them, although the larger ones would stay and watch you a bit longer.

The bats flew around the trees in the evening, some eating insects, others looking for fruit trees or blossums. In the mist you could see them by shining a torch, and they would fly through the beam of light, darting and weaving around with great agility. Night was also the time of the Echidna, or Spiny Anteater, to begin it's journey across the land searching for some ant or termite nests. Usually they were secretive, and the only sign we saw of them were large holes dug under logs or in the old termite mounds.

Sometimes one of the cats would go away for several days. Kitty was the most likely to do this, and we weren't sure where she went. Even in the winter, the weather didn,t bother her. The other three tended to stay put, and only ventured further afield occasionally. It wasn't really a big concern, as the cats were all quite big and strong enough to look after themselves. All the same, we did worry a bit sometimes.

We realize that we can't live forever on this earth. The cats can live for at least 15 years as a rule, if not a bit longer. They spend their time around us, and sometimes go for a walk. Anyway, it's good to have them around, along with our dog, and the various domestic birds, wildlife and so on. Hopefully in the future they will achieve a balance of some kind, and we will too. Who knows. As a domestic animal, our cats rely on us for their protection, if not their survival. They need a shelter from the storms as we do, something to eat, and a place to sleep. In fact, cats can spend 12 to 16 hours just sleeping. They often move around the house looking for a new spot, and might stay there for a few days before shifting to another place. They are usually quite self-sufficient, and independent from each other.

The cats would often play around the garden. One of their favourite games was to play chase around the Palm trees. Usually Cleo or Conrad would start a game, and the other two would follow. Tiga would often join in, and sometimes Kitty as well. The game usually involved one cat stalking the other, and then moving towards it, at which point the first cat would run behind the tree, followed by the other one. They would sometimes go around in circles at high speeds, and almost collide with another cat who stopped on one side of the tree. Sometimes they would suddenly race up the tree as well, and jump off somewhere else.

There were also some spectacular chases across the lawn, particularly between Conrad and Cleo. They enjoyed some wrestling matches, but weren't as interested in chasing a ball. Tiga started to bring small sticks and leaves into the house, so we tried to stop this. Eventually she understood not to do this. It may have had something to do with learning to hunt as well. Anyway, all the cats had a busy time as they grew up, and were generally friendly to each other!

20. Kitty goes walkabout.

One day Kitty disappeared for nearly two weeks. We were a bit worried at first, and as time went by we became more concerned. There were various reasons to be worried, as it was not exactly safe to just go roaming around in the outback.

Firstly, there was the problem of the wildlife. Cats may be hunters themselves, but their survival rate in the bush isn't exactly great. We only had one surviving cat, Kitty, from a litter of six kittens, and the mother cat had also passed away. There are many reasons why it is difficult for animals to survive in the wild. Sometimes they can, and other times they can't. To begin with, around our area are found the scrub ticks, which can be carried on a number of animals, or just found walking around on the ground. They can cause paralysis in cats and dogs. Then there were the Monitor Lizards, or Goannas which can prey on quite large animals. They are also adept at climbing ; I have seen big lizards race up quite large trees when they want to, and there were plenty of them down near the river.

In addition to this, there were various snakes, including some of the most deadly anywhere. The Pythons could strangle a small mammal, and would be happy to make a meal of a cat. The venemous snakes included the Eastern or King Brown snake and the Taipan, which are rated as No.2 and No.3 most deadly snakes in the world. There was also a Viper, and the Papuan Whip snake, and the Red-bellied Black snake, all of which had a venemous bite. After about two weeks and no sign of Kitty, we rang the Animal Refuge to report a missing cat, and I put up a notice, and we feared the worst.

KITTY COMES BACK - Amazingly, after two whole weeks with no sign of anything, Kitty suddenly appeared at the front door after dark. We heard a meeow, and there she was, looking a bit lean and hungry. The other cats didn't even seemed very surprised, as if they had known that she was just going away for a short time. Anyway, we were very happy to see her. She settled down inside the house again, and had a long sleep. I guess no one would know what adventures she had, or where she had been, except, of course, Kitty herself.

This wasn't the first time that Kitty had stayed away. But the other times it had only been for one, or two days at the most. The other cats were less adventurous. Tiga never went anywhere. Despite being the most camouflaged and a Tabby, she had no interest in going much further than our boundary fences. Cleo had stayed away one night, but hasn't repeated that again, and prefers to stay around the house. Conrad occasionally goes missing, but never for long. He is also happier to be around the house.

Cats are probably similar to dogs, in that they have a nomadic trait in them. This makes them a bit restless and means that they will travel a bit away from their homes for a while. This has happened to some of our animals in the past from time to time. It seems to be something which is built into them from the beginning, or from their birth, and it cannot really be changed. We don't know if one of our cats might go away again for a longer time, or where they might go for that matter, it can just happen. They might stay away for only a night, or two, or longer. If they can hunt they might get something to eat, otherwise they will certainly want to come back. Sometimes a cat might stay at another house for a while, or even swap houses with another cat! At least they can see fairly well in dim light.

21. Return of the Spring.

Following the winter, the spring was usually dry to begin with, and then the rains would come around Christmas. The dry grass would suddenly turn green, and plants flourished in the bush again. Our bird bath was always popular with the smaller birds, as well as the frogs. The Sunbird, which was like a kind of small honeyeater, would often dive into our pond for a wash, or sit in the bird bath. Sometimes a Magpie or a Butcherbird would sit in a tree watching below, and there were always Kookaburras around in their groups.

The flowering plants would also bring many insects. Beetles, Moths, Dragonflies and Butterflies could be seen at various times. At night the cats were interested in whatever crashed into the screen doors. Usually it was a grasshopper or a Katydid, or sometimes a large beetle. We often had diving beetles, as well as Rhinoceros beetles and dung beetles, and sometimes a Praying Mantis would sit on the wall, waiting to catch something to eat.

The Clohesy River flows through a forest near Koah.

The early spring and summer was a welcome change to the chilly days and low temperatures of the winter. It was also a time to plant. The farms had various crops which would grow well in the spring, and the rain was also welcome. Irrigation was important and vital to growing most of the time, and there were several different sources which people could use for this.

The main source for agriculture on the Tablelands was the irrigation from the dam called Lake Tinaroo. This supported many fruit farms and plantations, including Lychees, Bananas, Mangoes, Oranges and others. Some crops, such as Corn could be grown over the winter months, and were harvested in the spring, while others such as watermelons and pumpkins were harvested during the summer period. We set up an underground irrigation system for the various trees on our property, and also used sprinklers and hoses to keep the grass growing. Rainwater and river water were both used, and were often mixed together. There was considerable growth after heavy rain, and we did a lot of maintenance work trimming the trees and collecting fallen branches, especially from the Palm trees.

The river near our house, showing a sandbank and trees.

During the winter and spring, we were able to bring water up from the river using a pump. The water was generally clear, except when there was heavy rain, such as in the early summer and late autumn when the river would flood. We spent plenty of time keeping debris away from the inlet, and moving the pump before a flood.

Below : A collection of fish from the river, including Rainbowfish and Empire Gudgeons.
Right : A Jacaranda tree in flower.

For the cats, spring meant more warm days. Catching the sun in the morning was a favourite pastime, or sitting around outside anywhere even when it was hot. No one seemed to mind the sun. Only in the middle of the afternoon, when the sun was at really hot, did the cats and Leo our dog move into the shade. Otherwise they just stayed outside, basking in the warmth, or rolling in the sand.

They seemed to want a siesta at certain times of the day. It usually started around ten or eleven in the morning, and then they would come in at about three for a meal. Then they went back to rest until the evening, when they would decide to explore, or come back inside. Each cat was different, so they didn't always just follow the others. It could also depend on the weather conditions, although our cats didn't seem to mind the rain too much. If the rain was heavy, they would shelter on the porch or come back inside. Otherwise they would wait until the rain stopped falling, and go back outside again. Life was good, and there was always plenty of time anyway.

22. Guests and visitors.

From time to time other animals showed up on the property. We didn't mind this too much, however it depended on what they were actually doing here. A few wild cattle or even domestic ones which happened to find their way here, and roamed around in the fields wasn't a big deal, however if they started to munch our new trees around the lawn, that WAS a problem. We had seen what the Pigs and Kangaroos could do, and we had to be vigilant because most of the animals had ticks of one kind or another. The birds and the bats weren't too much of an issue, and we had the Frilled Lizards in the summer, but rarely the big Goannas.

We had a few wild ducks which landed in our dam, and stayed for a while. They even "shared" some of the chicken feed with our chooks, who weren't too impressed. A Peacock from our neighbours property also came and established himself in the tree, along with the Jungle Fowl and the Guinea Fowl. He was no trouble, and would often share some of the feed too. He had a loud call which resonated across the fields.

A Peacock displays his tail.

Conrad looks across the lawn at night.

It was, of course impossible to say what else had visited our farm at night. Occasionally there were signs of various things, such as tracks in the soft earth. It was easy to make out the tracks by the creek - the long slithers of the snakes, deep footprints of the Kangaroos, wild dogs or Dingoes, and so on. We had lost several of our chickens at night, even from inside the runs. Once we lost a big hen which had about seven chicks. We had to raise them ourselves by hand, but they all survived. That is life near the bush, to be sure.

The cats basically explored the area around our main house. They weren't so interested in venturing into the long grass. Perhaps they knew that there were hidden dangers like Taipans, or maybe it just wasn't that interesting. Their favourite occupations were to sit alongside the rows of coconut trees, or to try some climbing. There was always a thump when a coconut fell off a tree and hit an irrigation pipe. Not much we could do about it though, removing the coconuts would be too expensive for us. Plus we collected them and husked them to eat and make biscuits. I spent a lot of time repairing fences, but in the end we conceded that the animals ruled, so to speak. We could only try to discourage them a bit!

Cleo is one of our cats.

Leo is our dog.

23. The Future to come.

Sometimes it's fun to try and predict the future. Maybe even to look at things from an animals point of view. Maybe there will be more animal rights, maybe even in the United Nations. Who knows, maybe people will finally look after this planet and it's inhabitants.

Logically, we as humans are responsible for a lot of what happens on this planet. We may not be able to control things like the weather. If there is a drought, or a flood, we have to help each other to survive. Yet so do all the animals around us. They are also affected by the events of this planet in one way or another. There seems to be a balance in Nature which is sometimes changed, or affected by the actions of people. How complicated is this balance?

Perhaps some of the animals have a simpler way of seeing the world which has helped them to exist as they have for thousands of years. The ocean covers about two thirds of this planet, and has never been totally explored by mankind. Why do some animals, like the Dolphins try and help a human who is in trouble?

As terrestrial or land-based creatures we sometimes forget about the other forms of life around us. So what is there to learn from the animals? If we were as busy as the ants can be, we would probably get a lot of work done. To be as strong as a Lion or a Bear might be good too. Or maybe to be an Eagle which can fly as high as it likes, looking at the Earth below it. But we are not that strong, or busy, we are only humans who try and survive as best we can. And we can study the world around us and try to make sense of it all.

Not sure what our cats would think of the future, or their place in it. I guess they might consider where they could get a reasonable meal to eat, water to drink, and a good place as a shelter or a home. If dogs are family, why not the cats too? At least in some ways they have both existed with us for many years before today, as true domestic animals. And they can USUALLY live with us in our houses without too many problems, at least after they are trained.

" I wonder when it's going to start raining..."

Getting a cat like Kitty was a challenge as well as rewarding. Even though she was very young at first, she still had some habits which were quite typical of a wild cat. We just gave her food and shelter, and let her decide her own future. In the end she chose to stay with us, and at least spend most of her time at the house. The other cats were more attached to us because they had been born in the house, and grew up there too. Sometimes they were curious about Kitty, and wondered why she was so restless. It took time for her to settle down but now she is much happier. She still drinks milk, as do all our cats, and they prefer to eat Kangaroo meat except for Tiga who likes raw chicken and fish. Any other cat food is rejected. Our cats almost never catch birds, and I think that a cat which is well fed is a lot less likely to want go hunting, but you can never tell for sure. It's not a perfect world, but we all share it as a matter of course.

" One day I might be a movie star ..... I will be in the best movies, at all the great cinemas, and I will be rich and famous too! "

If cats were actors, they might take over Hollywood. They could run the studios, make the movies, organise promotions and previews, and maybe even include some humans as well as other animals in their films.

Cats like being in the great outdoors, so they would promote fitness and healthy living. They also like climbing, so they would encourage activities like trekking and climbing mountains.

If cats were involved in politics, they might make some new progress on transport - such as slowing down for animals and people, especially when they want to cross a road.

Cats may get some votes from people, but they might have trouble getting votes from some of the other animals, such as the mice and the small birds. This could be a stumbling block for them ....

If cats were involved with the media there would be more interesting and informative programs. There would be less commercials which interrupt what you want to watch, and more shows which are friendly towards animals and people too. Cats like eating so they would start some restaurants specializing in cat food and some other stuff too, and the world would be a better place to live.

Or maybe cats would just like to stay with their human friends like a big family. They might help us a bit, and in return we can offer them a place to stay and something to drink or eat. Yes, I don't know if cats would really like to run this world. And if they did, they would have to discuss and agree with everyone else, all the other animals, the humans, the fish in the sea and the bats and birds of the air. All the many animals from every corner and country of the world, big and small, the fierce and the friendly, the strong and the brave and the weaker ones would have to agree to support the rule of the Cats!

But the world goes on as usual, and people make most of the decisions about their lives, as well as what happens to the planet. And we can make a positive difference as well, even for the other beings who live on our planet. We are all different and unique, and this seems to be the case with most, if not all the animals too. As time goes by, we realize that our cats each have their own particular character traits and habits which we could never see before. They have grown into adults before us, yet they still group together like a small tribe, without much conflict at all. Who knows, maybe this is a sign for us as people in the future. Maybe we can learn something from their positive example, and those of other animals, if we only bother to look.

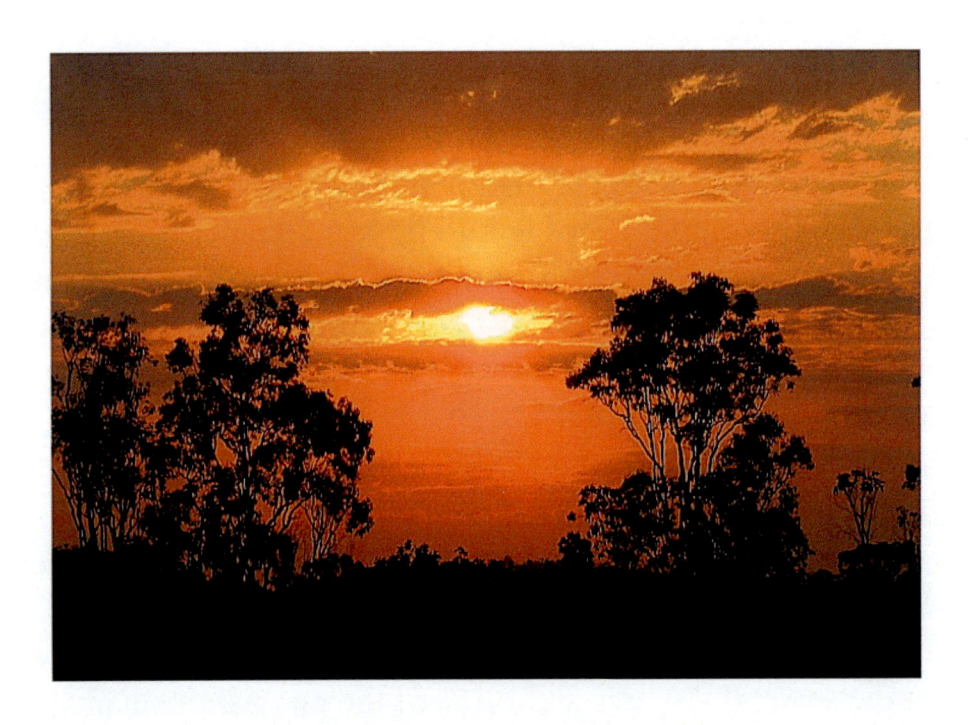

Made in the USA
Middletown, DE
09 December 2016